MARKS &
SPENCER

one-pot

simple and delicious easy-to-make recipes

Christine McFadden

Marks and Spencer p.l.c.
Baker Street, London, W1U 8EP

www.marksandspencer.com

Copyright © Exclusive Editions 2001

ISBN: 1-84273-002-9

Printed in China

Produced by The Bridgewater Book Company Ltd

COVER
Photographer Ian Parsons
Home Economist Sara Hesketh

NOTES FOR THE READER

- This book uses both metric and imperial measurements. Follow the same units of measurement throughout; do not mix metric and imperial.
- All spoon measurements are level: teaspoons are assumed to be 5 ml, and tablespoons are assumed to be 15 ml.
- Unless otherwise stated, milk is assumed to be full fat, eggs and individual vegetables such as potatoes are medium, and pepper is freshly ground black pepper.
- Recipes using raw or very lightly cooked eggs should be avoided by infants, the elderly, pregnant women, convalescents, and anyone suffering from an illness.
- Optional ingredients, variations or serving suggestions have not been included in the calculations. The times given are an approximate guide only. Preparation times differ according to the techniques used by different people and the cooking times may also vary.

contents

introduction

One-pot meals are the perfect solution for today's busy cooks. Whether it be a fortifying main-meal soup, an aromatic stew or casserole, or a hearty bake or gratin, a one-pot meal will look after itself while you do other things. They may not be fashionable food, but these are unpretentious, soul-satisfying dishes. They are also flexible as to timing, and can easily be kept waiting for late-comers. And in most recipes, leftovers can be reheated, to taste even better next time around.

Each of these dishes is a self-contained meal, needing little accompaniment – perhaps just a simple salad and a hunk of bread. Because the food is cooked and served in a single pot, you will not be confronted with a pile of dirty dishes either.

To cook on top of the stove, you will need a medium-to-large saucepan with a heavy flat base which prevents the contents from sticking and burning. Depending on the recipe, stove-top meals can also be prepared in a heavy-based, high-sided frying pan or sauté pan. For dishes that are started on top of the stove and finished in the oven, use a sturdy flameproof casserole or braising pan with ovenproof handles. All pans should have a well-fitting lid to keep the steam in and concentrate the flavours.

guide to recipe key		
	easy	Recipes are graded as follows: 1 pea = easy; 2 peas = very easy; 3 peas = extremely easy.
	serves 4	Recipes generally serve four people. Simply halve the ingredients to serve two, taking care not to mix imperial and metric measurements.
	20 minutes	Preparation time.
	1 hour	Cooking time.

speedy chilli beef
page 24

spicy chicken hot-pot
page 38

chickpea & potato curry
page 72

brazilian seafood stew
page 88

meat
one-pots

Thick, hearty soups such as Scotch Broth or Winter Minestrone with Sausage provide a nourishing meal-in-a-bowl, while the rich mellow flavours of traditional stews, such as Hungarian Goulash or Beef Bourgignon, will satisfy the most voracious of appetites. Chilli-lovers will enjoy Speedy Chilli Beef, as well as the robust spicy flavours of pork and beef in Mexican Meat Stew. There are also recipes for comforting casseroles and bakes with crisp toppings of garlicky breadcrumbs or bubbling cheese – perfect for a winter supper or weekend lunch.

winter minestrone
with sausage

		ingredients	
	easy	3 tbsp olive oil	1 small red pepper, seeded and diced
		250 g/9 oz coarse-textured pork	850 ml/1½ pints chicken stock
	serves 4	sausage, peeled and cut into chunks	salt and pepper
		1 onion, sliced thinly	50 g/1¾ oz short macaroni
		2 garlic cloves, chopped very finely	75 g/2¾ oz canned, drained
		200 g/7 oz canned chopped tomatoes	haricot beans
	30 minutes	2 tbsp chopped fresh mixed herbs,	115 g/4 oz frozen peas
		such as flat-leafed parsley,	2 tbsp freshly grated Parmesan, plus
		sage and marjoram	extra to serve
	40 minutes	1 celery stick, sliced thinly	4 thick slices ciabatta or French bread,
		1 carrot, diced	to serve

Heat the oil in a large saucepan over medium–low heat. Add the sausage and onion. Cook, stirring occasionally, until the onion is just coloured.

Add the garlic, tomatoes and herbs. Cook for 5 minutes, stirring. Add the celery, carrot and pepper, cover and cook for 5 minutes.

Pour in the stock. Bring to the boil, then cover and simmer gently for 30 minutes.

Season with salt and pepper. Add the macaroni and beans and simmer for about 15 minutes, or until the macaroni is just tender.

Stir in the peas and cook for 5 minutes more. Stir in the 2 tablespoons of Parmesan.

To serve, place the bread in individual serving bowls. Ladle the soup over the bread and leave to stand for a few minutes. Serve with plenty of freshly grated Parmesan.

ham and root soup

		ingredients	
easy		2 tbsp vegetable oil	800 g/1 lb 12 oz peeled root
		1 fresh bay leaf, shredded	vegetables, diced
serves 4		1 tsp finely chopped fresh rosemary	1 litre/1¾ pints chicken or ham stock
		200 g/7 oz piece of ham, diced	salt and pepper
		1 large onion, chopped finely	
20 minutes		2 celery sticks, diced	chopped fresh chives, to garnish
1 hour			

Heat the oil with the bay leaf and rosemary in a large saucepan over medium heat. Add the ham and stir-fry for a few minutes, or until beginning to crisp around the edges. Remove with a perforated spoon and set aside.

Add the onion, celery and root vegetables to the pan. Stir well, then cover and cook over a medium–low heat for 15 minutes.

Pour in the stock. Bring to the boil, then simmer, partially covered, for 30 minutes.

Purée about half the mixture in a blender or food processor, leaving the rest in the pan. Pour the purée back into the saucepan. Stir in the ham and cook over a medium–low heat until heated through.

Season with salt, bearing in mind the saltiness of the ham, and freshly ground black pepper. Sprinkle with chives and serve.

scotch broth

		ingredients	
	very easy	1 large onion, quartered	1 small celeriac, cut into chunks
		6 lamb shanks, weighing about	3 leeks, halved lengthways and
		1.6 kg/3 lb 8 oz	sliced thickly
	serves 6	1 head of garlic, unpeeled, the outer	3 sprigs fresh thyme
		loose layers removed	1 fresh bay leaf
		1 tbsp vegetable oil	1 tsp salt
	30 minutes	4 rashers unsmoked bacon, diced	1 tsp pepper
		1 large onion, diced	850 ml/1½ pints chicken or beef stock
		3 carrots, sliced	55 g/2 oz pearl barley
	2 hours 15 minutes	1 small swede, cut into chunks	4 tbsp chopped fresh parsley

Heat the oven to 230°C/450°F/Gas Mark 8. Roast the quartered onion, lamb and garlic in a roasting tin for 30 minutes, or until well browned, turning occasionally. Turn into a large heavy saucepan. Pour over water to cover. Slowly bring to the boil, skimming off any foam. Cook over a low heat, partially covered, for 1¼ hours.

Crisp the bacon in the oil in a large saucepan. Add the onion, vegetables, herbs and seasoning. Pour on the the stock and add the barley. Bring to the boil, then simmer 35–40 minutes.

Remove the lamb and garlic from the first pan with a perforated spoon. Strip the meat from the bones and squeeze out the garlic pulp. Line a sieve with kitchen paper. Strain the lamb cooking liquid into a bowl. Blot up any surface fat with kitchen paper. Add 700 ml/1¼ pints of the strained liquid, with the meat and garlic pulp, to the vegetables in the saucepan. Bring to the boil, then simmer for 10 minutes. Stir in the parsley just before serving.

mexican meat stew

		ingredients	
extremely easy		3 tbsp vegetable oil	125 ml/4 fl oz beef stock
		450 g/1 lb stewing beef, cubed	4 tbsp chopped fresh parsley
serves 4		450 g/1 lb boneless pork, cubed	1 tsp ground cumin
		1 onion, chopped finely	½ tsp dried oregano
		1 red pepper, seeded and chopped	½ tsp sugar
		2–4 green chillies, seeded and	salt and pepper
30 minutes		chopped finely	
		2 garlic cloves, chopped very finely	3 tbsp chopped fresh coriander,
		1.2 kg/2 lb 10 oz canned chopped	to garnish
3 hours		tomatoes	plain boiled rice, to serve
		3 tbsp lemon juice	

Heat the oil in a large flameproof casserole over a medium–high heat. Add the meat in batches and cook until browned on all sides. Remove each batch with a perforated spoon, transfer to a bowl and set aside.

Add the onion and pepper, and cook for 5 minutes, or until soft. Add the chillies and garlic, and cook until the garlic is just coloured. Return the meat and any juices to the casserole.

Add all the remaining ingredients, except the coriander. Bring to the boil, stirring. Cover and simmer over a low heat for 2 hours, stirring occasionally.

Remove the lid and simmer for 30–40 minutes, or until the sauce has thickened and the meat is very tender. Add more salt if necessary.

Garnish with the coriander just before serving. Serve with rice.

hungarian beef goulash

		ingredients	
extremely easy		2 tbsp vegetable oil	1 fresh bay leaf
		675 g/1 lb 8 oz stewing beef, cubed	3 tbsp chopped fresh parsley
serves 4		3 onions, chopped finely	1 tbsp paprika
		1 green pepper, seeded and diced	1 tsp salt
		2 garlic cloves, chopped very finely	¼ tsp pepper
		2 tbsp tomato purée	
30 minutes		2 tbsp plain flour	TO SERVE
		400 g/14 oz canned	buttered noodles
		chopped tomatoes	soured cream
3 hours		250 ml/9 fl oz beef stock	

Heat the oil in a flameproof casserole over a medium–high heat. Add the meat and fry until evenly browned. Remove with a perforated spoon, transfer to a bowl and set aside.

Add the onions and pepper. Cook for 5 minutes, stirring occasionally, until soft. Add the garlic and cook until just coloured. Stir in the tomato purée and flour. Cook for 1 minute, stirring continuously.

Return the meat to the pan. Add the remaining ingredients and bring to the boil. Cover and simmer over a low heat for 2½ hours, stirring occasionally. Add water or more stock if necessary.

Remove the lid and simmer for 15 minutes, stirring to prevent sticking, until the sauce has thickened and the meat is very tender.

Serve with buttered noodles and a bowl of soured cream.

beef bourguignon

		ingredients	
very easy		2 tbsp olive oil	700 ml/1¼ pints red wine
		175 g/6 oz piece unsmoked bacon, sliced into thin strips	350–450 ml/12–16 fl oz beef stock
serves 6		1.3 kg/3 lb stewing beef, cut into 5 cm/2 inch pieces	bouquet garni sachet
			1 tsp salt
		2 carrots, sliced	¼ tsp pepper
40 minutes		2 onions, chopped	3 tbsp butter
		2 garlic cloves, chopped very finely	350 g/12 oz pickling onions
		3 tbsp plain flour	350 g/12 oz button mushrooms
3 hours 15 minutes			2 tbsp chopped fresh parsley

Lightly brown the bacon in the oil in a large casserole (2–3 minutes). Remove with a perforated spoon. Brown the beef in batches, drain and keep with the bacon. Soften the carrots and chopped onions in the same pan for 5 minutes. Add the garlic and fry until just coloured. Return the meat and bacon to the pan. Sprinkle on the flour and cook for 1 minute, stirring. Add the wine and enough stock to cover, the bouquet garni, salt and pepper. Bring to the boil, cover and simmer gently for 3 hours.

Cook the pickling onions till soft in a covered frying pan in half the butter. Remove with a perforated spoon and keep warm. Fry the mushrooms in the remaining butter. Remove and keep warm.

Sieve the casserole liquid into a saucepan. Wipe the casserole and tip in the meat, bacon, mushrooms and onions. Remove the surface fat from the cooking liquid, simmer for 1–2 minutes to reduce, pour over the meat and vegetables. Serve sprinkled with parsley.

sausage
& tomato hotpot

		ingredients	
🖌	easy	2 tbsp olive oil	2 tsp chopped fresh rosemary
		225 g/8 oz coarse-textured pure pork	2 tsp chopped fresh thyme or oregano
		sausage, peeled and cut into chunks	1.2 kg/2 lb 10 oz canned
🍴	serves 4	2 onions, chopped finely	chopped tomatoes
		4 carrots, sliced thickly	salt and pepper
		6 potatoes, cut into chunks	
🥄	20 minutes	2 large garlic cloves, chopped	2 tbsp chopped fresh flat-leafed
		very finely	parsley, to garnish
🕐	1 hour		

Heat the oil in a large heavy-based saucepan over a medium–high heat. Add the sausage and fry until browned. Remove from the pan with a perforated spoon and set aside.

Reduce the heat to medium. Add the onions, carrots, potatoes, garlic, rosemary and thyme to the pan. Cover and cook gently for 10 minutes, stirring occasionally.

Return the sausage to the pan. Pour in the tomatoes and bring to the boil. Season with salt and pepper. Cover and simmer over a medium–low heat, stirring occasionally, for 45 minutes until the vegetables are tender.

Sprinkle with the parsley just before serving.

beef pot roast
with potatoes & dill

		ingredients	
	very easy	2½ tbsp plain flour	2 carrots, diced
		1 tsp salt	1 tsp dill seed
	serves 6	¼ tsp pepper	1 tsp dried thyme or oregano
		1.6 kg/3 lb 8 oz rolled brisket	350 ml/12 fl oz red wine
		2 tbsp vegetable oil	150–225 ml/9 fl oz beef stock
	40 minutes	2 tbsp butter	4 or 5 potatoes, cut into large chunks
		1 onion, chopped finely	and boiled till just tender
		2 celery sticks, diced	2 tbsp fresh dill to serve
	3 hours 30 minutes		

Mix 2 tablespoons of flour with the salt and pepper in a shallow dish. Dip the meat to coat. Heat the oil in a casserole and brown the meat all over. Transfer to a plate. Add 1 tablespoon of butter to the casserole and cook the onion, celery, carrots, dill seed and thyme for 5 minutes. Replace the meat and juices in the pan.

Pour in the wine and enough stock to reach one-third of the way up the meat. Bring to the boil, cover and cook for 3 hours in a preheated oven at 140°C/275°F/Gas Mark 1, turning every half hour. After 2 hours, add the potatoes and more stock if needed.

When ready, transfer the meat and vegetables to a warm serving dish. Sieve the cooking liquid into a saucepan.

Mix the remaining butter and flour to a paste. Bring the cooking liquid to the boil. Whisk in small pieces of the flour/butter paste, whisking until the sauce is smooth. Pour the sauce over the meat and vegetables. Sprinkle with the dill to serve.

speedy chilli beef

		ingredients	
extremely easy		3 tbsp vegetable oil	400g/14 oz canned red kidney beans,
		450 g/1 lb minced beef	drained and rinsed
serves 4		1 onion, chopped finely	1 tsp ground cumin
		1 green pepper, seeded and diced	1 tsp salt
		2 garlic cloves, chopped very finely	1 tsp sugar
15 minutes		800 g/1 lb 12 oz canned chopped	1–3 tsp chilli powder
		tomatoes	2 tbsp chopped fresh coriander
45 minutes			

Heat the oil in a large flameproof casserole over a medium–high heat. Add the beef and cook, stirring, until lightly browned.

Reduce the heat to medium. Add the onion, pepper and garlic. Cook for 5 minutes, or until soft.

Stir in the remaining ingredients, except coriander. Bring to the boil. Simmer over a medium–low heat, stirring frequently, for 30 minutes.

Stir in the coriander just before serving.

beef, mushroom
& rice casserole

		ingredients	
	extremely easy	3 tbsp olive oil	2 tbsp tomato purée
		400 g/14 oz minced beef	250 g/9 oz long-grain rice
	serves 4	1 onion, chopped finely	600 ml/1 pint hot beef stock
		1 pepper, seeded and chopped finely	salt and pepper
		150 g/5½ oz mushrooms, sliced	75 g/2¾ oz freshly grated Cheddar
	15 minutes		
	35 minutes		

Heat the oil in a high-sided lidded casserole over a medium–high heat. Add the beef and cook, stirring, until lightly browned.

Reduce the heat to medium. Add the onion, pepper, mushrooms and tomato purée. Cook for 5 minutes, or until soft.

Stir in the rice. Cook gently, stirring, for 3–4 minutes.

Pour in the hot stock. Season with salt and pepper. Bring to the boil. Cover tightly and simmer over low heat for about 20 minutes, or until the rice is tender and has absorbed most of the liquid.

Sprinkle with the cheese. Cover and leave to stand while the cheese melts. Serve at once, straight from the dish.

spanish ham
& rice one-pot

		ingredients	
very easy		2 tbsp olive oil	400 g/14 oz canned
		1 onion, chopped finely	chopped tomatoes
serves 4		1 red pepper, seeded and	200 g/7 oz long-grain rice
		chopped finely	450 ml/16 fl oz hot chicken stock
		350 g/12 oz piece of ham, cubed	salt and pepper
15 minutes		2 tsp paprika	85 g/3 oz frozen peas
35 minutes			

Heat the oil in a large heavy-based saucepan over a medium heat. Add the onion and pepper. Cook for 5 minutes, or until soft.

Stir in the ham, paprika, tomatoes and rice. Cook, stirring continuously, for 3–4 minutes.

Pour in the hot stock. Season with salt and pepper. Bring to the boil. Cover tightly and simmer over a low heat for 15 minutes.

Add the peas. Cover and cook for another 5 minutes, or until the rice is tender and has absorbed most of the liquid.

Remove the pan from the heat and leave the dish to stand for 5 minutes before serving.

lamb, garlic
& bean casserole

		ingredients
very easy		

serves 4	2 tbsp olive oil, plus extra for drizzling
	900 g/2 lb boneless lamb, cut into
	  4 cm/1½ inch cubes
	2 onions, chopped finely
	1 tbsp chopped fresh rosemary
	12 large garlic cloves, peeled and
	  left whole
	2 or 3 anchovy fillets, chopped
	  roughly
	2 tbsp plain flour
		½ tsp pepper
		600 ml/1 pint chicken or lamb stock
		225 g/8 oz dried cannellini or haricot
		  beans, soaked overnight and drained
		salt, to taste
		115 g/4 oz stale, coarse breadcrumbs
		
		chopped fresh flat-leafed parsley,
		  to garnish

45 minutes		
2 hours 30 minutes		

Heat 1 tablespoon of the oil in a flameproof casserole. When very hot, cook the lamb in batches until evenly browned. Transfer to a plate. Cook the onion and rosemary in the remaining oil in the casserole for 5–7 minutes, stirring, until golden brown. Reduce the heat, stir in the garlic and anchovies, and cook for 1 minute.

Preheat the oven to 150°C/300°F/Gas Mark 2. Return the meat and any juices to the casserole. Sprinkle with the flour and stir well. Season with the pepper. Pour in the stock, stirring continuously. Add the drained beans.

Bring to the boil, cover tightly and cook in the preheated oven for 2 hours, or until soft. Remove from the oven. Season with salt.

Spread the breadcrumbs over the lamb and beans. Drizzle a little olive oil over the top. Place under a preheated grill for a few minutes until the crumbs are golden brown. Sprinkle with parsley and serve immediately.

poultry one-pots

Versatile poultry forms the basis of a wealth of one-pot meals. Chicken features widely in appetising main-meal soups, spicy stews and hot-pots, and easily prepared bean and rice dishes. To get the taste buds tingling, try Spicy Chicken Hot-Pot or New Orleans-style Chicken Jambalaya. Sweet and meaty duck goes oriental in a richly flavoured stew of shiitake mushrooms and water chestnuts. Turkey is the main ingredient in what must be the speediest one-pot meal of all – a stir-fry of vibrant green mangetouts and pak choi.

chicken, squash & spinach soup

		ingredients	
easy		1 tbsp olive oil	400 g/14 oz canned chickpeas,
		1 tbsp butter	drained and rinsed
serves 4		3 boneless, skinless chicken breasts,	¼ tsp ground cumin
		cubed	salt and pepper
		2 small leeks, green part included,	1 litre/1¾ pints chicken stock
		sliced thinly	115 g/4 oz baby spinach, chopped
20 minutes		1 small butternut squash, cut into	coarsely
		2 cm/¾ inch cubes	
		1 small green chilli (optional), seeded	warm crusty bread, to serve
1 hour		and chopped very finely	

Heat the oil and butter in a large saucepan over a medium–low heat. Add the chicken, leeks, squash and chilli, if using. Cover and cook for 10 minutes, stirring occasionally, until the vegetables are beginning to soften.

Add the chickpeas, cumin, salt and pepper.

Pour in the stock. Bring to the boil, then simmer over low heat for 40 minutes, or until the squash is tender.

Stir in the spinach. Cook for a few more minutes until the spinach is just wilted, and serve with warm, crusty bread while piping hot.

chicken, sausage & bean stew

		ingredients	
easy		2 tbsp vegetable oil	¼–½ tsp dried chilli flakes
		4 boneless, skinless chicken breasts, cubed	400 g/14 oz canned chopped tomatoes
serves 4		225 g/8 oz coarse-textured pork sausage, cut into large chunks	400 g/14 oz canned cannellini beans, drained and rinsed
		4 frankfurter sausages, halved	150 ml/5 fl oz chicken stock
35 minutes		1 onion, chopped finely	salt and pepper
		3 carrots, sliced finely	
		1 garlic clove, chopped very finely	chopped fresh flat-leafed parsley,
45 minutes		1 tsp dried thyme	to garnish

Heat the oil in a large, heavy-based saucepan over a medium–high heat. Cook the chicken, pork sausage and frankfurters until lightly browned. Reduce the heat to medium. Add the onion and carrots. Cook for 5 minutes, or until soft.

Stir in the garlic, thyme and chilli flakes. Cook for 1 minute. Add the tomatoes, beans and chicken stock. Season with salt and pepper. Bring to the boil, then simmer over a low heat for 20–30 minutes, stirring occasionally.

Garnish with parsley just before serving.

spicy chicken hot-pot

very easy		**ingredients**
serves 4	2 tbsp vegetable oil	1 or 2 red chillies, deseeded and
	600 g/1 lb 5 oz skinless, boneless	chopped finely
	chicken breasts, cubed	1 tsp salt
	1 tsp cumin seeds, crushed	¼ tsp pepper
45 minutes	2 tsp coriander seeds, crushed	400 g/14 oz canned
	2 tsp dried oregano or thyme	chopped tomatoes
	1 onion, chopped	450 ml/16 fl oz chicken stock
	2 potatoes, cubed	175 g/6 oz green beans, cut
1 hour	2 sweet potatoes, cubed	into 4 cm/1 ½ inch pieces
15 minutes	3 carrots, sliced thickly	8 x frozen sweetcorn cob quarters
	3 garlic cloves, chopped very finely	chopped fresh coriander, to garnish

Heat the oil in a casserole over a medium–high heat. Cook the chicken until lightly browned, stirring frequently. Stir in the cumin, coriander and oregano. Cook for 1 minute.

Reduce the heat to medium. Add the onion, potatoes, sweet potatoes, carrots, garlic and chillies. Cover and cook for 10 minutes, stirring occasionally, until beginning to soften.

Add the salt and pepper. Pour in the tomatoes and stock. Bring to the boil, cover and simmer over a medium–low heat for 30 minutes.

Add the beans and sweetcorn. Cook for 15 minutes more, or until the beans are just tender.

Garnish with coriander just before serving.

chicken, beans & spinach with olives

		ingredients
very easy		
		2 tbsp olive oil
serves 4		600 g/1 lb 5 oz skinless, boneless
		chicken breasts, cut into chunks
		1 small onion, chopped finely
		2 celery sticks, diced
20 minutes		3 large garlic cloves, chopped finely
		2 tsp chopped fresh rosemary
		¼ tsp dried chilli flakes
45 minutes		400 g/14 oz canned
		chopped tomatoes

Ingredients (right column):

400 g/14 oz canned cannellini beans,
   drained and rinsed
250 ml/9 fl oz chicken stock
salt and pepper
350 g/12 oz baby spinach,
   chopped roughly

8–10 pitted black olives (sliced),
   to garnish

Heat the oil in a casserole over a medium–high heat. Cook the chicken until lightly browned, stirring frequently.

Reduce the heat to medium. Add the onion and celery. Cook for 5 minutes, or until soft.

Stir in the garlic, rosemary and chilli flakes. Cook for another minute. Add the tomatoes, beans and chicken stock. Season with salt and pepper.

Bring to the boil, then simmer over a medium–low heat for 20 minutes. Stir in the spinach. Cook for about 3 minutes, or until wilted.

Garnish with the olives and serve immediately.

chicken with rice, mushrooms & tomatoes

	very easy	
	serves 4	
	15 minutes	
	1 hour	

ingredients

2 tbsp olive oil
650 g/1 lb 7 oz boneless, skinless
  chicken breasts, cubed
1 onion, chopped finely
115 g/4 oz mushrooms, sliced finely
2 garlic cloves, chopped very finely

4 tbsp chopped fresh flat-leaf parsley
350 g/12 oz long-grain rice
400 g/14 oz canned
  chopped tomatoes
salt and pepper
450 ml/16 fl oz hot chicken stock

Heat the oil in a large heavy-based frying pan over a medium–high heat. Cook the chicken until lightly browned, stirring frequently.

Reduce the heat to medium. Add the onion and mushrooms. Cook for 5 minutes, or until soft. Stir in the garlic and 2 tablespoons of the parsley. Cook for 1 minute.

Add the rice and cook for 5 minutes, stirring constantly. Add the tomatoes. Season with salt and pepper. Cook for another minute. Stir in the hot stock. Bring to the boil, then cover tightly and simmer over a low heat for 20–25 minutes, or until the rice is tender.

Remove from the heat and leave the dish to stand, covered, for 10 minutes before serving. Sprinkle with the remaining parsley to garnish and serve.

chicken jambalaya

		ingredients	
easy		3 tbsp vegetable oil	1 tsp dried oregano
		900 g/2 lb boneless, skinless chicken	¼ tsp dried chilli flakes
serves 4		thighs	225 g/8 oz chorizo sausage,
		1 onion, chopped finely	cut into chunks
		2 red or green peppers, seeded and	3 plum tomatoes, chopped roughly
		chopped finely	salt and pepper
30 minutes		2 garlic cloves, chopped very finely	600 ml/1 pint hot chicken stock
		300 g/10½ oz long-grain rice	3 spring onions, green part included,
		2 tbsp tomato purée	chopped finely
1 hour 10 minutes		1 tsp dried thyme	

Heat the oil in a flameproof casserole over a medium–high heat. Cook the chicken in batches until lightly browned, stirring frequently. Remove with a perforated spoon and transfer to a plate.

Reduce the heat to medium. Add the onion and peppers. Cook for 5 minutes, or until soft. Add the garlic and cook for 1 minute. Add the rice and cook for 5 minutes, stirring constantly.

Add the tomato purée, thyme, oregano, chilli flakes, chorizo and tomatoes. Season with salt and pepper. Cook for 2–3 minutes.

Return the chicken and any juices to the casserole. Stir in the hot stock. Bring to the boil, then cover tightly and simmer over low heat for 20–25 minutes, or until the rice is tender.

Remove from the heat. Sprinkle with the spring onions. Cover and leave to stand for 10 minutes before serving.

braised oriental duck

		ingredients	
	very easy	3 tbsp soy sauce	1 tbsp oyster sauce
		¼ tsp Chinese five-spice powder	3 whole star anise
		¼ tsp pepper; pinch of salt	2 tsp black peppercorns
	serves 4	4 duck legs or breasts, cut into pieces	450–600 ml/16 fl oz–1 pint chicken
		3 tbsp vegetable oil	stock or water
		1 tsp dark sesame oil	6 dried shiitake mushrooms, soaked in
	30 minutes	1 tsp finely chopped ginger root	warm water for 20 minutes
		1 large garlic clove, finely chopped	225 g/8 oz canned water chestnuts,
		4 spring onions, white part sliced	drained
	2 hours	thickly, green part shredded	2 tbsp cornflour
		2 tbsp rice wine or dry sherry	

Combine 1 tablespoon of the soy sauce, five-spice powder, pepper and salt and rub over the duck pieces. Brown the duck pieces in 2½ tablespoons of vegetable oil, remove and transfer to a plate.

Drain the fat from the casserole and wipe out. Heat the sesame oil and remaining vegetable oil. Add the ginger and garlic. Cook for a few seconds. Add the white spring onion. Cook for a few seconds. Return the duck to the pan. Add the rice wine, oyster sauce, star anise, peppercorns and remaining soy sauce. Pour in enough stock to just cover. Bring to the boil, cover and simmer gently for 1½ hours, adding more water if necessary.

Drain the mushrooms and squeeze dry. Slice the caps and add to the duck with the water chestnuts. Simmer for 20 minutes more.

Mix the cornflour with 2 tablespoons of the cooking liquid to a smooth paste. Add to the remaining liquid, stirring until thickened. Garnish with the green spring onion shreds to serve.

turkey stir-fry
with noodles

		ingredients	
easy		225 g/8 oz dried egg noodles	115 g/4 oz mangetouts,
		250 g/9 oz turkey escalopes,	halved lengthways
serves 4		cut into thin strips	225 g/8 oz pak choi, cut into
		1 tsp cornflour	1 cm/½ inch diagonal slices
		1 tsp sugar	6 thin slices fresh ginger root,
20 minutes		¼ tsp salt	chopped very finely
		3 tbsp soy sauce	1 large garlic cloves chopped
		3 tbsp vegetable oil	very finely
20 minutes		2 tbsp dark sesame oil	salt and pepper
		6–8 shiitake mushrooms, sliced finely	

Cook the noodles according to the packet instructions. Drain, rinse with cold water and set aside.

Spread the turkey strips on a plate. Dredge with the cornflour, sugar, salt and soy sauce. Toss well to coat.

Heat 2 tablespoons of vegetable oil and 1 tablespoon of sesame oil in a wok or large frying pan over high heat. When very hot, add the turkey. Stir-fry for 2 minutes. Add the mushrooms, mangetouts and pak choi. Stir-fry for 2 minutes. Add the ginger and garlic. Stir-fry for 1 minute. Season with salt and pepper. Transfer the turkey and vegetables to a warm dish.

Reduce the heat to medium. Add the remaining oils to the pan. When hot, add the cooked noodles. Stir-fry for 2 minutes, or until heated through and coated with oil. Return the turkey and vegetables to the pan. Mix with the noodles and serve at once.

mexican chicken, chilli & potato pot

		ingredients	
	easy	2 tbsp vegetable oil	1 or 2 fresh green chillies, seeded and
		450 g/1 lb boneless, skinless	chopped very finely
	serves 4	chicken breasts, cubed	200 g/7 oz can chopped tomatoes
		1 onion, chopped finely	½ tsp dried oregano
		1 green pepper, seeded and	½ tsp salt
		chopped finely	¼ tsp pepper
	30 minutes	1 potato, diced	4 tbsp chopped fresh coriander
		1 sweet potato, diced	450 ml/16 fl oz chicken stock
	35 minutes	2 garlic cloves, chopped very finely	

Heat the oil in a large heavy-based saucepan over a medium–high heat. Cook the chicken until lightly browned.

Reduce the heat to medium. Add the onion, pepper, potato and sweet potato. Cover and cook for 5 minutes, stirring occasionally, until the vegetables begin to soften.

Add the garlic and chillies. Cook for 1 minute. Stir in the tomatoes, oregano, salt, pepper and 2 tablespoons of the coriander. Cook for 1 minute.

Pour in the stock. Bring to the boil, then cover and simmer over a medium–low heat for 15–20 minutes, or until the chicken is cooked through and the vegetables are tender.

Sprinkle with the remaining coriander just before serving.

paprika chicken
& rice casserole

		ingredients	
easy	3 tbsp vegetable oil	450 ml/16 fl oz hot chicken stock
	4 part-boned chicken breasts,	2 tsp paprika
serves 4	about 150 g/5½ oz each	2 tsp dried thyme
	1 onion, chopped finely	salt and pepper
	2 garlic cloves, chopped very finely	175 g/6 oz Cheddar or mozzarella,
20 minutes	200 g/7 oz long-grain rice	coarsely grated
	280 g/10 oz frozen mixed vegetables	
1 hour		

Heat the oil in a shallow flameproof casserole a over medium–high heat. Cook the chicken in batches until lightly browned. Remove with a perforated spoon and transfer to a plate.

Reduce the heat to medium. Add the onion. Cook for 5 minutes until soft. Add the garlic and cook for 1 minute. Stir in the rice and cook for 5 minutes, stirring constantly.

Add the frozen vegetables, the hot stock, 1 teaspoon each of the paprika and thyme. Bring to the boil, stirring until well mixed. Season with salt and pepper. Place the chicken breasts on top of the rice mixture. Sprinkle with the remaining paprika and thyme.

Cover tightly and simmer over low heat for 20–25 minutes, or until the liquid is absorbed and the chicken cooked through.

Remove from the heat. Sprinkle with the cheese. Place under a preheated grill for 5 minutes. Serve when the cheese has melted.

turkey, leek
& cheese gratin

		ingredients	
easy		115 g/4 oz short macaroni	225 g/8 oz diced cooked turkey
		1 small egg, beaten lightly	or chicken
serves 4		2 tbsp butter	55 g/2 oz diced ham
		4 small leeks, green part included,	3 tbsp chopped fresh
		sliced finely	flat-leafed parsley
30 minutes		2 carrots, diced	salt and pepper
		1 tbsp plain flour	100 g/3½ oz freshly grated
		¼ tsp freshly grated nutmeg	Gruyère cheese
40 minutes		250 ml/9 fl oz chicken stock	

Cook the macaroni in plenty of boiling salted water until just tender. Drain and return to the pan. Stir in the egg and a knob of the butter, mixing well. Set aside.

Preheat the oven to 180°C/350°F/Gas Mark 4.

Melt the remaining butter in a saucepan over medium heat. Add the leeks and carrots. Cover and cook for 5 minutes, shaking the pan occasionally, until just tender.

Add the flour and nutmeg. Cook for 1 minute, stirring constantly. Pour in the stock. Bring to the boil, stirring constantly. Stir in the turkey, ham and parsley. Season with salt and pepper.

Spread half the turkey mixture over the base of a shallow baking dish. Spread the macaroni over the turkey. Top with the remaining turkey mixture. Sprinkle with the cheese.

Bake in the preheated oven for 15–20 minutes. Serve when the cheese is golden and bubbling.

vegetable
one-pots

Vibrant vegetables combine with the earthy flavours of pulses, grains and pasta in deeply satisfying and nutritious one-pot meals. All are simple to prepare and make exciting eating whatever the occasion – midweek suppers, or entertaining friends. Try Barley and Pepper Pilaf, or the colourful and crisp-textured Lentil and Rice Pilaf with Celery, Carrots and Orange – perfect for a festive vegetarian meal. Or experience the earthy, complex flavours of mushrooms and aubergines in Baked Mediterranean Vegetables with Feta.

hearty lentil
& vegetable soup

		ingredients	
	very easy	2 tbsp vegetable oil	75 g/2¾ oz long-grain rice
		3 leeks, green part included,	1 litre/1¾ pints chicken stock
		sliced finely	8 x sweetcorn cob quarters
	serves 4	3 carrots, diced	salt and pepper
		2 celery sticks, quartered lengthways	
		and diced	TO SERVE
	15 minutes	115 g/4 oz brown or green lentils	4 tbsp chopped fresh chives
			soured cream
	40 minutes		

Heat the oil in a large saucepan over medium heat. Add the leeks, carrots and celery. Cover and cook for 5–7 minutes, or until just tender. Stir in the lentils and rice.

Pour in the stock. Bring to the boil, then cover and simmer over a medium–low heat for 20 minutes.

Add the sweetcorn. Simmer for 10 minutes more, or until the lentils and rice are tender.

Season with salt and pepper. Stir in the chives. Ladle into individual bowls, top with a spoonful of soured cream and serve immediately.

beans & greens soup

		ingredients	
	very easy	3 tbsp olive oil	400 g/14 oz canned borlotti beans,
		1 large white onion, sliced thinly	drained and rinsed
	serves 4	3 garlic cloves, chopped very finely	850 ml/1½ pints chicken or
		2 or 3 mild green chillies, such as	vegetable stock
		Anaheim, seeded and chopped	salt and pepper
	30 minutes	1 tsp dried oregano	
		250 g/9 oz shredded savoy cabbage	3 tbsp chopped fresh coriander,
		or kale	to garnish
	20 minutes		

Heat the oil in a large saucepan over a medium heat. Cook the onion for 5–7 minutes or until soft.

Add the garlic, chillies and oregano. Cook for a few seconds, or until the garlic is just beginning to colour. Add the cabbage, beans and stock. Season with salt and pepper.

Bring to the boil, then cover and simmmer for 7–10 minutes or until the cabbage is just tender.

Sprinkle with the coriander just before serving.

creamy potato, onion & cheese soup

		ingredients	
	very easy	3 tbsp butter	150 ml/5 fl oz milk
		1 small onion, chopped finely	150 ml/5 fl oz whipping cream
	serves 4	6 spring onions, green part included, chopped finely	3 tbsp chopped fresh parsley
			75 g/2¾ oz coarsely grated Cheddar
		4 potatoes, cut into chunks	
	15 minutes	700 ml/1¼ pints chicken stock	fried garlic croûtons (optional),
		salt and pepper	to serve
	30 minutes		

Heat the butter in a large saucepan over medium heat. Add the onion, spring onions and potatoes. Cover and cook for 5–7 minutes until the onions are just tender.

Add the stock. Bring to the boil, then cover and simmer over a medium–low heat for 15–20 minutes, or until the potatoes are tender. Remove from the heat.

Mash the potatoes. Season with salt and pepper. Stir in the milk, cream and 2 tablespoons of the parsley. Reheat gently. Ladle into bowls. Sprinkle with the cheese and remaining parsley.

Serve with the croûtons, if using.

tomato, mushroom & macaroni hot-pot

		ingredients	
	easy	3 tbsp olive oil	800 g/1lb 12 oz canned
		1 onion, sliced	chopped tomatoes
	serves 4	75 g/2¾ oz mushrooms, sliced thinly	450 ml/16 fl oz chicken stock
		2 garlic cloves, chopped very finely	225 g/8 oz dried short macaroni
		1 tsp dried oregano	1 tsp salt
		2 tbsp tomato purée	¼ tsp pepper
	20 minutes	3 tbsp chopped fresh	
		flat-leaf parsley	freshly grated Parmesan, to serve
	30 minutes		

Heat the olive oil in a large saucepan or high-sided frying pan with a lid, over medium heat. Add the onion and mushrooms. Cook, stirring for 5–7 minutes, or until soft.

Stir in the garlic, oregano, tomato purée and 1½ tablespoons of the parsley. Cook for 1 minute. Pour in the tomatoes and stock. Bring to the boil.

Add the macaroni, salt and pepper. Bring back to the boil. Cover and simmer over a medium–low heat for 20 minutes, stirring occasionally, or until the macaroni is tender.

Sprinkle with the remaining parsley just before serving. Serve with freshly grated Parmesan.

mexican three-bean chilli hotpot

		ingredients	
	very easy	140 g/5 oz each black beans, cannellini beans and pinto beans, soaked overnight in separate bowls	½–2 tsp chilli powder
			3 tbsp tomato purée
	serves 6		800 g/1 lb 12 oz canned chopped tomatoes
		2 tbsp olive oil	
		1 large onion, chopped finely	1 tsp sugar
		2 red peppers, seeded and diced	1 tsp salt
	30 minutes	2 garlic cloves, chopped very finely	600 ml/1 pint chicken or vegetable stock
		½ tsp cumin seeds, crushed	
		1 tsp coriander seeds, crushed	3 tbsp chopped fresh coriander
	2 hours	1 tsp dried oregano	

Drain the beans, put in separate saucepans and cover with fresh water. Boil rapidly for 10–15 minutes, then simmer for 35–45 minutes, or until just tender. Drain and set aside.

Heat the oil in a large heavy-based saucepan, over a medium heat. Cook the onion and peppers for 5 minutes, or until soft.

Stir in the garlic, cumin and coriander seeds, and oregano. Cook for a few seconds, or until the garlic is just beginning to colour. Add the chilli powder and tomato purée. Cook for 1 minute. Add the tomatoes, sugar, salt, beans and stock. Stir well and bring to the boil. Cover and simmer over a low heat for 45 minutes, stirring occasionally to prevent sticking.

Stir in the coriander and remove from the heat. Ladle into individual bowls to serve.

barley & pepper pilaf

easy	
serves 4	
25 minutes	
1 hour 15 minutes	

ingredients

1 tbsp vegetable oil
2 tbsp butter
1 onion, chopped finely
1 red pepper, deseeded and
  chopped finely
1 green pepper, deseeded and
  chopped finely

225 g/8 oz mushrooms, sliced thinly
2 tbsp chopped fresh flat-leaf parsley
2 garlic cloves, chopped very finely
125 g/4½ oz pearl barley
400–600 ml/14 fl oz–1 pint chicken
  or vegetable stock
salt and pepper

Heat the oil and butter in a high-sided frying pan with a lid over medium heat. Add the onion, peppers and mushrooms. Cook for 5–7 minutes, or until soft, stirring often.

Add the parsley and garlic. Cook for 1 minute. Add the barley and mix well. Pour in 400 ml/14 fl oz of the stock. Season with salt and pepper.

Stir, bring to the boil, then cover and simmer over a low heat for about 1 hour, or until the barley is tender and most of the liquid has been absorbed. Add more stock if necessary.

Remove from the heat and leave to stand for 5 minutes. Fluff with a fork before serving.

lentil & rice pilaf
with celery, carrots & orange

		ingredients	
	very easy	4 tbsp vegetable oil	40 g/1½ oz whole almonds, sliced
		1 red onion, chopped finely	lengthways
	serves 4	2 tender celery sticks, leaves included,	350 g/12 oz cooked brown
		quartered lengthways and diced	basmati rice
		2 carrots, grated coarsely	150 g/5½ oz cooked orange lentils
	30 minutes	1 green chilli, seeded and chopped	175 ml/6 fl oz chicken or vegetable
		finely	stock
		3 spring onions, green part included,	5 tbsp fresh orange juice
	15 minutes	chopped finely	salt and pepper

Heat 2 tablespoons of the oil in a high-sided frying pan with a lid over a medium heat. Add the onion. Cook for 5 minutes, or until soft.

Add the celery, carrots, chilli, spring onions and almonds. Stir-fry for 2 minutes, or until the vegetables are al dente but still brightly coloured. Transfer to a bowl and set aside.

Add the remaining oil to the pan. Stir in the rice and lentils. Cook over a medium–high heat, stirring, for 1–2 minutes, or until heated through. Reduce the heat. Stir in the stock and orange juice. Season with salt and pepper.

Return the vegetables to the pan. Toss with the rice for a few minutes until heated through. Transfer to a warm dish to serve.

chickpea & potato curry

		ingredients	
	easy	225 g/8 oz chickpeas, soaked	½ tsp cayenne
		3 tbsp vegetable oil	2 tbsp tomato purée
		½ tsp cumin seeds	400 g/14 oz canned chopped
	serves 6	½ tsp mustard seeds	tomatoes
		1 onion, chopped finely	2 potatoes, cubed
		2 garlic cloves, chopped very finely	3 tbsp chopped fresh coriander
	40 minutes	2 cm/¾ inch piece fresh ginger root,	1 tbsp lemon juice
		chopped very finely	250–300 ml/9–10 fl oz chicken or
		1 tsp salt	vegetable stock
	2 hours	2 tsp ground coriander	thinly sliced white or red onion rings,
		1 tsp turmeric	and cooked rice, to serve

Boil the chickpeas rapidly in plenty of water for 15 minutes. Reduce the heat and boil gently for 1 hour, or until tender. Drain and set aside.

Heat the oil in a large saucepan or high-sided frying pan. Stirring all the time, add the cumin and mustard seeds, cover and cook for a few seconds, or until the seeds pop. Add the onion. Cover and cook for 3–5 minutes, or until just brown. Add the garlic and ginger. Cook for a few seconds. Stir in salt, coriander, turmeric and cayenne, then the tomato purée and tomatoes. Simmer for a few minutes. Add the chickpeas, potatoes and 2 tablespoons of the coriander.

Stir in the lemon juice and 250 ml/9 fl oz of the stock. Bring to the boil, then simmer for 30–40 minutes, or until the potatoes are cooked. Add stock if the mixture becomes too dry.

Serve garnished with onion rings and the remaining coriander.

baked mediterranean vegetables with feta

		ingredients	
very easy		1 red onion, sliced into thick rings	1 tbsp chopped fresh flat-leaf parsley
		1 small aubergine, sliced thickly	1 tsp chopped fresh rosemary
serves 4		2 large mushrooms, halved	1 tsp dried thyme or oregano
		3 red peppers, halved, cored and	finely grated zest of 1 lemon
		seeded	75 g/2¾ oz stale, coarse breadcrumbs
		3 tbsp olive oil, plus extra for brushing	6–8 black olives, pitted and sliced
40 minutes		3 plum tomatoes, peeled and diced	25 g/1 oz feta, cut into
		salt and pepper	1 cm/½ inch cubes
		2 garlic cloves, chopped very finely	
40 minutes			

Put the onion, aubergine, mushrooms and peppers on a large baking tray, placing the peppers cut side down. Oil lightly.

Grill for 10–12 minutes, turning the onion, aubergine and mushroom halfway through, until beginning to blacken. Cut into even-sized chunks. Place in a shallow ovenproof dish. Arrange the diced tomatoes on top. Season with salt and pepper.

Preheat the oven to 220°C/425°F/Gas Mark 7.

In a bowl, combine the garlic, parsley, rosemary, thyme and lemon peel with the breadcrumbs. Season with pepper. Add the 3 tablespoons of olive oil to bind the mixture together. Scatter the mixture over the vegetables. Add the olives and feta cheese.

Bake in the preheated oven for 10–15 minutes, or until the vegetables are heated through and the topping is crisp. Serve straight from the dish.

spinach, mushroom & rice gratin

		ingredients	
easy		1 tbsp olive oil	salt, to taste
		1 tbsp butter	450 g/1 lb spinach, stalks removed,
serves 4		1 onion, chopped finely	leaves sliced into thin ribbons
		225 g/8 oz mushrooms, sliced finely	200 g/7 oz long-grain rice
		2 garlic cloves, chopped very finely	400 ml/14 fl oz water
35 minutes		½ tsp dried thyme or oregano	¼–½ tsp pepper
		¼ tsp dried chilli flakes	115g/4 oz Edam or mild Cheddar,
		finely grated zest of ½ lemon	coarsely grated
50 minutes			

Heat the oil and butter in a large saucepan over medium heat. Add the onion and mushrooms. Cook for 5 minutes, or until soft. Add the garlic, thyme, chilli flakes, lemon peel and salt to taste. Cook for a few seconds.

Add the spinach and stir until wilted. Stir in the rice and cook for a few minutes, or until the grains are translucent. Add the water and bring to the boil. Cover tightly and simmer over a low heat for 15–20 minutes, or until the water has been absorbed.

Preheat the oven to 180°C/350°F/Gas Mark 4.

Transfer the mixture to a lightly greased ovenproof baking dish. Season with the pepper. Sprinkle the cheese over the surface. Gently fork it into the rice.

Cover with foil. Bake in the preheated oven for about 20 minutes, until the cheese has melted.

Remove the foil and bake for 5 minutes more before serving.

aubergine gratin

		ingredients
very easy		4 tbsp olive oil
serves 4 as a starter		2 onions, chopped finely
15 minutes		2 garlic cloves, chopped very finely
40 minutes		2 aubergines, sliced thickly
		3 tbsp chopped fresh flat-leaf parsley
		½ tsp dried thyme

ingredients

4 tbsp olive oil
2 onions, chopped finely
2 garlic cloves, chopped very finely
2 aubergines, sliced thickly
3 tbsp chopped fresh flat-leaf parsley
½ tsp dried thyme

salt and pepper
400 g/14 oz canned
  chopped tomatoes
175 g/6 oz mozzarella,
  coarsely grated
6 tbsp freshly grated Parmesan

Heat the oil in a frying pan over a medium heat. Add the onion and cook for 5 minutes, or until soft. Add the garlic and cook for a few seconds, or until just beginning to colour. Using a perforated spoon, transfer the onion mixture to a plate.

Cook the aubergine slices in batches in the same pan until they are just lightly browned.

Preheat the oven to 200°C/400°F/Gas Mark 6.

Arrange a layer of aubergine slices in the base of a shallow ovenproof dish. Sprinkle with some of the parsley, thyme, salt and pepper. Add a layer of onion, tomatoes and mozzarella, sprinkling parsley, thyme, salt and pepper over each layer.

Continue layering, finishing with a layer of aubergine slices. Sprinkle with the Parmesan. Bake, uncovered, in the preheated oven for 20–30 minutes, or until the top is golden and the aubergines are tender. Serve hot.

fish
one-pots

Easy to prepare and quick to cook, fish and
seafood make mouthwatering one-pot
meals. Fresh or frozen, bottled or canned,
a variety of fish and seafood can go into
the pot. Firm-fleshed white fish, such as cod
or snapper, are ideal since they maintain
texture and succulence while gently
simmering in a sauce. Plump, juicy prawns,
briny clams, scallops and mussels also
provide a taste of the ocean. The recipes
include a Brazilian seafood stew, redolent
with saffron, as well as rich, creamy
chowders and a Cajun-style gumbo.

seafood chowder

		ingredients	
	very easy	1 tsp vegetable oil	salt and pepper
		4 rashers streaky bacon	1.2 litres/2 pints hot milk
	serves 4	4 tbsp butter	350 g/12 oz firm white fish,
		1 large onion, chopped finely	such as cod, haddock or hake,
		2 celery sticks, quartered lengthways	cut into chunks
		and diced	280 g/10 oz clams (in jar)
	40 minutes	3 floury potatoes, cubed	6–8 peeled tiger prawns, halved
		3 tbsp chopped fresh parsley	6 large scallops (optional),
		1 tsp chopped fresh thyme	sliced thickly
	40 minutes	1 fresh bay leaf	

Heat the oil in a frying pan over a medium–high heat. Cook the bacon until crisp. Drain on kitchen paper, crumble into bite-sized pieces and set aside.

Heat the butter in a large saucepan. Add the onion, celery and potatoes. Reduce the heat to medium–low. Cover and cook for 10 minutes, stirring occasionally, until beginning to soften.

Add 2 tablespoons of the parsley, the thyme and bay leaf. Season generously with salt and pepper. Pour in the hot milk. Cover and simmer for 15 minutes. Add the fish and continue cooking for 5 minutes.

Add the clams and their juice, the prawns and scallops, if using. Simmer for 5 minutes more.

Ladle into individual bowls. Serve garnished with the bacon pieces and the remaining parsley.

caribbean fish chowder

		ingredients	
	very easy	3 tbsp vegetable oil	salt and pepper
		1 tsp cumin seeds, crushed	400 g/14 oz red snapper fillets,
	serves 4	1 tsp dried thyme or oregano	cut into chunks
		1 white onion, diced	25 g/1 oz frozen peas
		½ green pepper, seeded and diced	25 g/1 oz frozen sweetcorn kernels
		1 sweet potato, diced	125 ml/4 fl oz single cream
	35 minutes	2 or 3 green chillies, seeded and	
		very finely chopped	3 tbsp chopped fresh coriander,
		1 garlic clove, chopped very finely	to garnish
	45 minutes	1 litre/1¾ pints chicken stock	

Heat the oil with the cumin seeds and thyme in a large saucepan over a medium heat. Add the onion, pepper, sweet potato, chillies and garlic. Cook, stirring, for 1 minute.

Reduce the heat to medium–low. Cover and cook for 10 minutes, or until beginning to soften.

Pour in the chicken stock. Season generously with salt and pepper. Bring to the boil, then cover and simmer over a medium–low heat for 20 minutes.

Add the red snapper, peas, sweetcorn and cream. Cook, uncovered, for 7–10 minutes, or until the fish is cooked.

Stir in the coriander to garnish just before serving.

prawn gumbo

		ingredients	
very easy		2 tbsp vegetable oil	1 fresh bay leaf
		2 tbsp butter	salt and pepper
serves 4		250 g/9 oz okra, trimmed and	850 ml/1½ pints chicken stock
		sliced thickly	or water
		1 white onion, chopped finely	450 g/1 lb fresh or frozen raw prawns,
		2 celery sticks, quartered lengthways	shelled
40 minutes		and diced	few drops of Tabasco sauce
		1 green pepper, seeded and diced	
		2 garlic cloves, chopped very finely	2 tbsp chopped fresh coriander,
45 minutes		200 g/7 oz canned chopped tomatoes	to garnish
		½ tsp dried thyme or oregano	

Heat the oil and butter in a large saucepan over a medium heat. Add the okra and cook, uncovered, for 15 minutes, or until it loses its gummy consistency.

Add the onion, celery, pepper, garlic, tomatoes, thyme and bay leaf. Season with salt and pepper. Cover and cook over a medium–low heat for 10 minutes.

Pour in the stock. Bring to the boil, then cover and simmer over a medium–low heat for 15 minutes, or until the vegetables are al dente. Add the prawns and Tabasco sauce. Cook for about 5 minutes, or until the prawns are pink.

Stir in the coriander to garnish just before serving.

brazilian seafood stew

		ingredients	
easy		450 g/1 lb mussels, scrubbed	salt and pepper
		2 tbsp olive oil	900 g/2 lb cod steaks, cut into chunks
serves 4		1 onion, chopped finely	225 g/8 oz raw tiger prawns, peeled
		2 garlic cloves, chopped very finely	200 g/7 oz canned crab meat
		400 g/14 oz canned	200 g/7 oz clams (in jar)
		chopped tomatoes	
30 minutes		¼ tsp cayenne	3 tbsp chopped fresh coriander,
		pinch of saffron threads	to garnish
35 minutes			

Remove the 'beards' from the mussels. Rinse the mussels well, to remove any sand, and discard any with broken shells or that remain open when tapped.

Heat the oil in a large saucepan or flameproof casserole over a medium heat. Add the onion and cook for 5 minutes, or until soft.

Stir in the garlic, tomatoes, cayenne and saffron. Season with salt and pepper. Cook for 5 minutes, stirring occasionally.

Add the cod and the cleaned mussels. Pour in enough water to just cover and bring to the boil. Reduce the heat to low. Cover and simmer for 10 minutes, or until the mussels open. Discard any that have not opened.

Add the prawns, crab meat and clams with their juice. Simmer for 5 minutes more, or until the prawns are pink.

Stir in the coriander just before serving.

chunky cod stew
with celery & peppers

		ingredients	
easy		2 red peppers, halved, cored and seeded	salt and pepper
			2 celery sticks, sliced finely
serves 4		3 tbsp olive oil	600 g/1 lb 5 oz fresh or frozen thick
		1 onion, chopped finely	cod steaks, cut into chunks
		2 garlic cloves, chopped very finely	55 g/2 oz stale coarse breadcrumbs
		1 tbsp white wine vinegar	8–10 black olives, pitted and sliced
35 minutes		1 tbsp tomato purée	
		1 tbsp dried thyme or oregano	chopped celery leaves, to garnish
		250 ml/9 fl oz fish stock	
1 hour 10 minutes			

Place the peppers cut side down on a baking tray under a preheated hot grill for 10–12 minutes until beginning to blacken. Heat 1 tablespoon of the olive oil in a shallow casserole. Cook the onion for 5 minutes, stirring. Add the garlic, vinegar, tomato purée and half the thyme or oregano. Cook, stirring, for 1 minute. Add the stock. Simmer for 5 minutes.

Preheat the oven to 200°C/400°F/Gas Mark 6. Remove the skin from the peppers. Roughly chop the flesh. Put in a blender or food processor with the onion mixture. Season with salt and pepper. Purée until smooth and pour into the casserole. Add the celery and cod. Bring to the boil, then cover and bake in the preheated oven for 35 minutes.

Combine the breadcrumbs, remaining oil, olives, remaining thyme, salt and pepper in a small bowl. Sprinkle over the fish. Brown under a hot grill for 5 minutes. Garnish with chopped celery leaves before serving.

monkfish ragoût

		ingredients	

easy		2 tbsp olive oil
		1 small onion, chopped finely
		1 red pepper, seeded and cut into
		   2.5 cm/1 inch pieces
		115 g/4 oz mushrooms, sliced finely
		3 garlic cloves, chopped very finely
		1 tbsp tomato purée
		2 tbsp chopped fresh
		   flat-leafed parsley
		½ tsp dried oregano
			400 g/14 oz canned
			   chopped tomatoes
			150 ml/5 fl oz dry red wine
			salt and pepper
			550 g/1 lb 4 oz monkfish, skinned
			   and cubed
			1 yellow or green courgette, sliced
			
			6–8 fresh basil leaves (shredded),
			   to garnish

serves 4–6			
35 minutes			
35 minutes			

Heat the oil in a heavy-based saucepan or flameproof casserole over a medium heat. Add the onion, pepper and mushrooms and cook for 5 minutes, or until beginning to soften.

Stir in the garlic, tomato purée, parsley and oregano.
Cook together for 1 minute. Pour in the tomatoes and wine.
Season with salt and pepper. Bring the mixture to the boil, then simmer gently for 10–15 minutes, or until slightly thickened.

Add the monkfish and the courgette slices. Cover and simmer for 15 minutes, or until the monkfish is cooked and the courgette is tender but still brightly coloured.

Sprinkle with the basil just before serving.

seafood hotpot with
red wine & tomatoes

		ingredients	
	very easy	350 g/12 oz mussels, scrubbed	225 ml/8 fl oz dry red wine
		4 tbsp olive oil	salt and pepper
	serves 4–6	1 onion, chopped finely	450 g/1 lb firm white fish,
		1 green pepper, seeded and chopped	such as cod or monkfish, cut into
		2 garlic cloves, chopped very finely	5 cm/2 inch pieces
		5 tbsp tomato purée	115 g/4 oz scallops, halved
	40 minutes	1 tbsp chopped fresh	115 g/4 oz raw prawns, shelled
		flat-leafed parsley	200 g/7 oz can crab meat
		1 tsp dried oregano	
	1 hour 10 minutes	400 g/14 oz canned	10–15 fresh basil leaves, shredded,
		chopped tomatoes	to garnish

Remove the 'beards' from the mussels. Rinse the mussels well,
to remove any sand, and discard any with broken shells or that
remain open when tapped.

Heat the oil in a heavy-based saucepan or flameproof casserole
over a medium heat. Add the onion and pepper. Cook for
5 minutes, or until beginning to soften.

Stir in the garlic, tomato purée, parsley and oregano. Cook for
1 minute, stirring.

Pour in the tomatoes and wine. Season with salt and pepper.
Bring to the boil, then cover and simmer over a low heat for
30 minutes. Add the fish. Cover and simmer for 15 minutes.

Add the mussels, scallops, prawns and crab meat. Cover and cook
for 15 minutes more. Discard any mussels that have not opened.

Stir in the basil just before serving.

index